Shigeo Kikuchi

# Memoirs of a

# BUDDHIST WOMAN MISSIONARY

# in Hawaii

## Shigeo Kikuchi

**BUDDHIST STUDY CENTER PRESS**
An outreach of the Shin Buddhist Temples of Hawaii
HONPA HONGWANJI MISSION

Library of Congress Cataloging-in-Publication Data

Kikuchi, Shigeo.
    [Kaikyō shoki no omoide. English]
    Memoirs of a Buddhist woman missionary in Hawaii /
    Shigeo Kikuchi
  ; translated by Florence Okada.
        p.     cm.
    Translation of: Kaikyō shoki no omoide.
    ISBN 0-938474-13-8  :  $6.95
    1. Kikuchi, Shigeo.  2. Priests, Buddhist--Hawaii--Wives-
-Biography.  3. Shin (Sect)--Missions--Hawaii.  4. Women,
Buddhist--Hawaii--Biography.  5. Shin Buddhists--Hawaii-
-Biography.
BQ968.I43A3      1991
294.3'926--dc29                                        91-2906
[B]                                                        CIP

Copyright © 1991 Florence Okada

Available from: The Buddhist Study Center Press
1727 Pali Highway, Honolulu, Hawaii 96813

# Acknowledgements

I WISH TO express my deep gratitude to Mrs. Evelyn Shimizu, Dr. George Tanabe, Rev. Yoshiaki Fujitani, Mrs. Bertha Nishida and to the many others who helped in so many ways with this tranlation.

Florence Okada
Honolulu, 1991

# About the Translator

MISS FLORENCE OKADA did this sensitive English translation from the original Japanese text edited after Mrs. Kikuchi's death by Rev. Hiromi Kawaji of Wailuku, Maui. Like Mrs. Kikuchi, who was her dear friend, Miss Okada has devoted her life to Buddhist service in the spirit of the nembutsu. In 1938, on the recommendation of the eminent late scholars Professors Kiritani and Joen Ashikaga, she completed studies in Japan and received ordination as a Shin Buddhist minister *(tokudo)*. For much of her career she was a Japanese Language teacher at Fort Gakuen in Honolulu and a dharma school teacher at Hawaii Betsuin. In this translation she continues her life work of spreading the dharma of the nembutsu teaching of Shinran Shonin.

# About This Book

In 1991 the slogan for Hongwanji in Hawaii is "Every person ministry", a contemporary way of emphasizing our founder Shinran's description of himself as "neither monk nor lay." A Hongwanji Buddhist minister is, primarily, a dharma teacher - one who spreads the nembutsu teaching of Amida Buddha's fulfilled vow and its universal endowment of buddhahood.

To spread the dharma is, essentially, the mission of each Buddhist and has been so since Sakyamuni Buddha decided to 'turn the wheel of the law' by sharing the truth of his enlightenment with others.

In Shin Buddhism, the mission is neither intrusive nor aggressive. It is a quietly natural way of conducting one's life, relating to others, and doing whatever possible in however small a way to help make this turbulent world a Pure Land, a realm of enlightenment, peace, and joy with no discrimination, no distinctions, no prejudice, and no violence, exploitation, aggression or suppression.

By this Buddhists do not yearn to create some idealistic Utopia. They are simply carrying on the working of Amida's Vow, in which wisdom and compassion is realized as the fundamental basis of all existence, and buddhahood - enlightenment - the unconditional endowment of every one and every thing, throughout the universe.

It is both in this sense of Hongwanji's 'every person ministry' as 'every person missionary' and in tribute to the very special role of bomori - minister's wives past and present that we have chosen for the title of these poignant recollections of a pioneer bomori in Hawaii, "Memoirs of a Buddhist Woman Missionary in Hawaii".

Shigeo Kikuchi, in this book, provides not only a rare portrait of the caring, giving life of a bomori but also records a very important, previously undocumented picture of life in the first half of the twentieth century in rural plantation Hawaii.

It is with deep gratitude to bomori like the late Shigeo Kikuchi, author of this book, to Buddhist women missionaries like its translator, Florence Okada of Hawaii Betsuin, and Jane Imamura, widow of Hawaii's former Bishop Kanmo Imamura (who so graciously wrote the following preface) that Buddhist Study Center Press presents this twelfth in its series of books on Shin Buddhism in and for everyday life in this New Age.

The Press is deeply indebted to Buddhist Study Center's Director, Rev. Yoshiaki Fujitani, (whose mother was also an outstanding bomori in the history of Hongwanji in Hawaii) for his guidance and support both as former Bishop and as current Director of Buddhist Education.

Ruth Tabrah, Editor
Buddhist Study Center Press

# Preface

IN THE HAWAII *Kaikyoshi* published in 1918, it is written: "in 1911, Principal Rev. Chikyoku Kikuchi, and faculty, Shigeo Kikuchi tended to the Naalehu Hongwanji Japanese Language School where 64 children gathered." These were the struggling pioneer days of Hawaii, where the land and languages were alien, where racial barriers were high, where the searing sun burned on the plantations, and where there was endless work to be done.

In this hostile environment, we can picture the gentle figures of the couple, settling in Naalehu in 1907. Except for short stints on Kauai and Maui, and separation during WWII when Mrs. Kikuchi tended to the temple alone while her husband was taken away by the FBI to be interned on the mainland, they, with single-minded dedication worked for the Buddha, Dharma and Sangha until his retirement in 1953. The couple had also administered to Pahala Hongwanji, and were instrumental in building the temples and sangha in both areas. The patience and diligence of losing themselves in their work for forty-odd years in one place is remarkable, especially to our present day yardstick, when technology has accelerated us to expect instant gratifications. Now, even 10 years seems a lifetime. I can remember a year more recently, when there was talk in the Giseikai about 5 year rotating terms for the ministers.

Long-term commitment like that of the Kikuchi's was the way of life in those days. The Rev. H. Miyasaki's who came to Hawaii in 1903 spent their lives in Lihue and worked for forty-five years. The Rev. C. Miyagawa's came in 1904 and immersed themselves for even longer. There are too many names to recount here of ministers and *bomoris* who became stepping stones just so that we, the younger generations, may receive the greatest treasure, that of the dharma.

In 1967 when my husband became the Bishop in Hawaii, Mrs. Kikuchi visited him often. I sensed an indescribable communion between them, for surely, she felt in him his father, the former Bishop Y. Imamura, with whom so many of the early ministers and *bomoris* worked side by side. For those pioneer ministers and *bomori* alike, it was a hard life. They were living a true non-ego life. . .without concern for their own lives. Shigeo Kikuchi was of small physical stature, but her vast experiences emanated around her.

However, in 1976, watching her frail figure leaving the Bishop's residence, I could not help but feel a certain tinge of sadness.

Someone said, "The priests in Japan live an unchanging life of rice paddies, while ministers in America live a life of sheep." In Japan, the priest is born and dies in his temple and generations of his family continue in the same temple. But in America, a minister is a nomad. Like a sheep herder, he moves from one temple to another. A permanent home or the luxury of a pension seem to have never entered the minds of the early ministers. I do not know how Mrs. Kikuchi fared after her husband died. I know that she moved away from Naalehu. For a time, she joined her son in Chicago. But I suspect the snowy weather, the industrial environment and non existence of a Japanese community must have been difficult. Those of us *bomoris* born in America are more fortunate. We can find jobs, drive and live relatively comfortably.

Professor Sosuke Nishimoto once wrote, "A thought that refuses to leave me, is about the lives of ministers' widows who are living out their lives in America." There are many widowed *bomoris* living quietly in America. Through this book we are reminded of their sacrifices, and offer gassho (a gesture of respect and reverence) to them. Their selfless pioneering in Hawaii almost a century ago, through accounts like this journal, will help future generations to understand the beginnings of their heritage in Hawaii.

Jane Imamura
Berkeley, California

BSC

# Coming to Hawaii

SEVEN YEARS AFTER my husband had left for Hawaii I boarded an ocean-liner, the Shun'yo Maru, from Yokohama. After sailing for ten days, I reached Hawaii and landed at Honolulu in May, 1914. At that time Japanese hotels were centered around Beretania Street. They were the Kobayashi Hotel, Yamashiro Hotel, and other hotels where most of the Japanese visitors stayed. Along the Main street downtown, stores were lined in rows and city transportation was by horse cart. The Hawaii Betsuin, a wooden structure, was located about two blocks toward downtown from the present temple on lower Fort Street (now Pali Highway). Waikiki in those days consisted of rice and taro fields, and human dwellings were rare. I only stayed for three days in Honolulu, then went on to Wailuku Hongwanji on Maui, where my husband was the resident minister.

Wailuku Hongwanji stood within an area of about 7,200 square feet. There was a main temple worship hall and the minister's living quarters. It was a very quiet location. In the back of the worship hall was the two-story house used for the minister's quarters. It had a parlor, dining room and kitchen on the first floor. However, the floor was of rough wood and

1

adjacent to the living quarters (kuri) were a horse stable and garage.

I arrived at Wailuku Hongwanji temple at the time of the celebration honoring the birthday of our founder, Shinran Shonin. In addition to this Gotan'e Service, there was popular entertainment. I can say that my life as a minister's wife started with this event commemorating Shinran Shonin's birthday. Members of the temple built a stage within the temple grounds to welcome me to Wailuku Hongwanji. People from various social strata who lived in the neighborhood welcomed me so warmly that I remember to this day being deeply moved by the event, as though it had occurred only a few days ago.

Wailuku is located in central Maui, therefore many visitors came from all directions and I was kept busy entertaining them. In addition, in the mornings, afternoons, and evenings I taught at the Japanese language school. On Saturday it was especially busy because the teaching hours were longer than those on weekdays. On Sunday there was Dharma school and many other activities. My husband and I both taught the Japanese language, therefore, no matter how tired I was, I could not ask him to relieve me. My husband tried not to teach evening classes because when he had to travel long distances for Buddhist services, he also had to care for his horse afterwards. (Whenever he took the horse and cart he was away for a long time.) So I walked six times a week from the temple and our living quarters which was in the south of Wailuku town to the school, which was in the north section.

When we had visitors, the temple took care of their meals because at Wailuku there weren't any good restaurants. Since I would be late for school if I cleaned up after the meals, there were many times I left the dirty dishes on the table. One day when I came home very tired, I saw my dining table all cleared and cleaned. Later I learned that Mrs. Tamiko Egami, who had a candy shop nearby, came to my home during a break from her busy schedule to help clean up the dishes on the table.

My husband went to distant plantation areas to conduct services and returned home late practically every night. After he took off the saddle from the horse and saw that everything was in good condition, then we had our dinner. Sometimes I also returned home late, and on those occasions our dinner time was very late. This situation continued for a while, until one day Dr. Oyama's wife, who lived next door, called us saying, "Bath and dinner are ready, please come over." We accepted her kind words and favors without any hesitation. I shall never forget the kindness of that couple. From then on, we inconvenienced them many times. My husband played Japanese checkers (Go) with Dr. Oyama, while Mrs. Oyama and I traded stories about Japan. Our warm friendship with the Oyamas made us forget the busyness in our lives.

As a matter of reference, I should say that the district of Wailuku Hongwanji included Wailuku plantation, Kahului, Kihei, and Waikapu. A branch temple was in Kahului. In all, there were about two thousand Japanese residents in those areas. The Wailuku Hongwanji status report of that time included, besides the Gojikai (supporting membership); the Women's Club (Fujinkai) which numbered Wailuku, 95; Kahului, 26; Waikapu, 39; the YBA, 32 members; Sunday School, 160 pupils; and the Japanese Language School, 204 students. My husband, the Reverend Chikyoku Kikuchi was the superintendent, and Mr. Risuke Yasui was the principal. The teachers were Takeko Matsumura, Kiyoko Yasui, Kuroda Sensei and myself—six teachers in all. The classes lasted one hour in the morning, two hours in the afternoon, and there were also night classes from Monday to Saturday, six days a week. Every year the school sponsored

3

a play for two nights and three days in order to accrue funds to pay the debts for the new school building fund. The profit from these plays paid all the debts. I still feel a deep emotion when I remember the happy faces of the people who shouted "Banzai" and recited the nembutsu with their hands folded in gassho at the party to celebrate the completion of the paying off of the debts.

Not long after residing at Wailuku Hongwanji, I was accompanied by my husband and visited the Hongwanji Cemetery to pay my respects to the pioneers buried there. My husband said that there were about nine hundred deceased members, including the late Reverend Hojun Kunizaki, the first minister of Wailuku Hongwanji who died while actively serving his people. Listening to many stories of the past, I was impressed by the early pioneers' spirit that overcame the hardships and struggles of the past, and thus, brightened the present Hongwanji.

Days and months passed like a dream with the many miscellaneous duties of a minister's wife. One day Dr. Oyama warned me, "Mrs. Kikuchi, it seems that you have lost weight. Please take good care of your body." Although I was unbearably homesick for Japan, my extremely busy daily schedule probably helped me to forget my homesickness.

Both my husband and I loved people. We welcomed daily callers and much enjoyed visitors coming from far away. Also we were happy to see young men freely coming to our minister's quarters. These gatherings of dharma friends were a full-time program. Although I say our daily routine was busy, there were times when I enjoyed going on outings with YBA club members and also with the Women's club to Iao Valley or to the beach. So there were many fruitful days when we felt that our work was not burdensome. However, there was such a difference between my husband's income and our

4

expenditures, that no matter how hard I tried to cut down on our living expenses, the social expenses increased and our debts grew. I was getting quite familiar with Wailuku, when one day Mr. Yasui, President of Maui Shimbun, said, "Mrs. Kikuchi, if you don't economize and if you do not pay up your debts within three years you will be a hated person and your husband will be useless as a minister." I was forced to consider his warning very seriously. (Of course, I paid our debts as promised.)

Surrounded by the good wishes of many people, we had finally grown accustomed to Wailuku. Suddenly the day came for us to bid farewell to Maui. We received a letter from Bishop Yemyo Imamura asking us if we would transfer immediately. I was against this transfer but my husband accepted it. The reason for this transfer was that the daughter of the Reverend and Mrs. Toda, the resident minister of Naalehu, became ill and died because there was no doctor living in Naalehu. As parents they could not bear to have this happen again to their other children. The Rev. Toda, therefore, requested a transfer to a place where there was a doctor and a hospital. He said that if this was not possible, he would resign and go back to Japan. Knowing this, the members of Naalehu asked to have Reverend Kikuchi as their minister. By this time my husband had been a resident minister at Wailuku for three years but I had hardly been there for a full year. I could not insist on my preference to stay, so we accepted the transfer.

To my husband Naalehu was surely a deeply karma-related place. His first assignment as a minister in Hawaii, for four years from 1907 to 1910, was a Naalehu and Pahala. But to me Naalehu was a completely unknown world. The day I left Wailuku, I kept thinking of Reverend Kunizaki.

# Naalehu

AFTER DEPARTING FROM Wailuku Hongwanji we paid our respects at Hilo Hongwanji on the way to Naalehu. From Hilo we rode on a five passenger Ford car at a speed of twenty miles an hour for seventy miles, on a narrow, uneven road to Naalehu. Nine miles from Hilo we reached Olaa, a small country town with a Hongwanji temple and a camp of fourteen to fifteen white, lime-coated houses all in rows. After passing the camp, there were no more houses to be seen, nothing but cane fields until we came to the Volcano House. Along the road-side on the way were beautiful alpine flowers. The view from the hotel of the crater, with smoke rising from between the streams of lava was most impressive.

However, after passing through this scene, again there was nothing but cane fields and pastures, not even a car came along and this lonely journey continued. Mr. Kawamura, president of the temple, and Mr. Kono, an advisor of Naalehu Hongwanji, were old acquaintances of Rev. Kikuchi. They were together in the car chatting and laughing on the way to Naalehu. I alone felt lonely and miserable. Before long we came to the district of Ka'u and approached a narrow road that passed between the Pacific Ocean on one side and a small hill on the other. This road had seven bad curves. When two cars met, one had to wait at a place so that the other car could pass through. It was such an inconvenient and dangerous narrow road! At last, after this, we soon reached Naalehu Hongwanji, where we were welcomed by the members of the temple.

After paying respects at the main worship hall, I was ushered to the minister's living quarters. I was surprised to find the walls and floors were made of rough wood and the outside was coated with white lime. A white cloth was spread under the ceiling to prevent lizard droppings and dust from falling. There were no electric lights. Lamps were used. To go out at night, lanterns were used. The toilet, which was not the flushing type, was outside of the house. Even at Wailuku I had been homesick, but now I was put completely in a different environment than that of Wailuku. I was so disappointed! I was even resentful of my husband because he had consented to this transfer to Naalehu without consulting me. My tears flowed, but when I thought about Reverend Kunizaki I tried to get back my courage. I heard that in Naalehu there was no minister's quarter at first. The members through their hard work were able to build this simple residence.

Seven years ago, when my husband was first assigned to Naalehu, he fell off his horse while he was on his way to give a sermon. He was critically injured and for eight months he was between life and death. Because he was single, the camp people took good care of him in this same room. However, at that time there was not even a ceiling. When I heard this from my husband suddenly I felt awfully ashamed for having had such extravagant dreams. When I realized this, my mind turned to a new direction and I was determined to live my life more strongly.

Besides Naalehu Hongwanji the propagation areas in those days were divided into thirteen camps. The furthest camps were twelve to thirteen miles away from the temple, so to go to these camps and return home from services was physically taxing. At certain places visited by my husband, his greeting of "Good Evening," sometimes was met with abuse. Some people would say, "The priest has come, throw salt at him!" Or they would say, "We are having a 'tanomoshi' meeting so come some other time," and his entry was refused. The horse was the only means of transportation, but the temple was so poor that it was almost impossible to even keep a horse.

My husband surely suffered from poverty. Besides the temple duties at Naalehu, there was more miscellaneous work than at Wailuku. For instance, I had to write letters or birth reports for others, help with procedures for returning to Japan, make deposits at the bank, and besides, I had to teach Japanese Language School, which kept my husband and me pretty busy. However, it also made our personal relationships closer and more intimate.

As days and months passed, I became accustomed to Naalehu. Visitors and guests increased. Therefore, one of the rooms was turned into a guest room. The ceiling and the surrounding walls were fixed. Naalehu was just half way from Hilo to Kona. Travelers would reach Naalehu about noon but in Naalehu there were no restaurants nor hotels to accommodate them. Many well-known people from various places stopped and rested for lunch. In some cases the travelers requested a lodging for the night so it became necessary to have a room for these guests. The guest room also served as our bedroom but whenever we had a guest we moved our bed to another room. I was concerned about this kind of situation and as a minister's wife I took great care of outside guests and visitors. My husband understood my feelings, but my duties as a housewife simply piled up. In this time of no radio and television, we country people were fortunate to have the chance to listen to many educational and cultural stories from guests and visitors.

The population of Naalehu in those days was approximately fifteen hundred Japanese, one thousand Filipinos, and five hundred Hawaiian, haoles, and Portuguese. Of this number about eight hundred Japanese worked at the sugar mill between 1898 and 1905, which was the most prosperous period for the Japanese communities.

Besides Naalehu Hongwanji, the other missionary districts were such areas as Waiohinu, Honuapo, Hiilea, Miss Taylor camp, and Portuguese House. Besides these areas, there were separate camps such as Miyauchi camp, Mauka Makai Waiubata, Kawalaiki Ninole, Wailau, Kaalualu, Waihokena, the Luna's House, and Pahala Group. After Japanese school was over, my husband picked up his horse from the stock-farming pasture and got ready to go to these camps practically every day for propagation. He made every effort to spread the Dharma, never complaining of his unending tasks. With a feeling of gratitude toward him, I vowed to help ease my husband's burden and worries by teaching school, taking care of guests and doing various work besides my dharma duties. It was unthinkable either to make idle complaints or take things for granted. For my husband and for me, it was a rigorous life, with a schedule which was busier than that at Wailuku.

In those days, except for the three Japanese who managed stores, most of the resident Japanese were engaged in working in the sugar cane fields. Both husband and wife worked together to earn a living. Only the people who lived in Honuapo Mill camp worked at the sugar plantation mill.

9

Women who lived near the Naalehu temple worked as washing women for haoles or for the single men. Some lived as domestic workers for haoles. At camp, there was a place called "Big Cook" where a person was contracted to serve three meals a day to single men.

Washing clothes in those days was strenuous work because they used soap and washed by hand on a washing board. The clothes that were soiled by dirt and perspiration could not be easily cleaned, so they used an empty kerosene can, put soap into the water, and boiled them to remove the dirt. They dried the clothes during the day and at night they ironed the clothes using an iron heated with charcoal. The price of washing clothes for single men was $2.00 a month. On the plantation women worked for 58 cents a day. In terms of being busy and poor, our everyday living was not much different from that of the laborers. When I think of the time spent for our social and other duties and the great hardships suffered I am sure that I would not have been able to survive that life without the nembutsu.

# Things Worth Remembering

HERE I HAVE something worth writing about. Men and women in those days worked very hard, and it was a fact that they were always worried about their children's future. Another striking thing about these people was that they did not forget their native homeland of Japan. One day Mrs. S.'s daughter said to me, "Sensei, my mother told my sister, Kazuesan, that whenever school is on vacation always to go to the temple to help sensei and while you are helping her learn good things. This is what mother always used to say. No matter how busy we were at home, sister Kazue was always sent to sensei's home."

Ordinarily parents sent their children to a place where they would receive an income. At times when parents needed the most help children did not go to school but instead worked at home. Sometimes children were sent out to some other homes to work in order to lessen their food expenses. However, Mrs. S.'s case was different. She had ten children, Kazue was the first, the eldest daughter, and was already in the eighth grade. Her parents needed Kazue the most for helping at home because despite their ten young children, Mrs. S. and her husband both worked in the cane fields.

Indeed, in their household, even the proverbial hand of a cat was needed. Since Kazue was already in the eighth grade, she would have been of great help at home taking care of her younger brothers and sisters. In spite of all this, she was allowed to keep her regular school hours and in addition was sent to help at the temple to learn 'even one good deed to benefit herself.'

Hearing this, I said, "Kazuesan, is this so? Is this your mother's intention?" I was so deeply moved by her parents' love that I could not hold back my tears. Parents like Mrs. S. who in those days worked at the plantation took their breast feeding child to work, put them under the shade of a tree beside the field and let them sleep there. It was common for the mother to rush to her infant during the rest breaks to nurse. They earned only 58 cents a day but still they had to endure such contract work to help feed their family.

When the children became of school age, parents woke up very early to prepare meals for their children. Before going to work in the cane fields, they took their children on horse-back and dropped them off at Naalehu. Two miles from Naalehu the children went to Waiohinu public school, where they first received their English lessons. After public school was over they hastened to Japanese school, rushing and sweating in the afternoon heat so as not to be late. They said that even if there were guavas on the trees on the way to Japanese school they had no time to pick and eat them. After giving them their lessons in Japanese every day for one hour and seeing them return to their homes, I felt they were so loveable that I forgot my own tiredness. This helped me to keep up with my work.

The distance between the Japanese school and their homes was far, so children waited for their fathers to pick them up. As soon as the children heard the approach of horse's hoofsteps on the road, the expressions on their faces grew exceptionally happy. Whenever I saw this, I felt so happy and thankful for the preciousness of our teacher-student relationship.

These children had no chance of listening to everyday English conversation of the Caucasians - the haoles. They were brought up by their Japanese-speaking parents. Their friends and playmates often spoke different prefectural dialects plus a mixture of Hawaiian words. It may be in this connection that such incidents as the following occurred at the public school in Naalehu because the children did not understand what their teachers were telling them.

One day I just happened to pass by the first grade classroom as the teacher was asking, "What happened to you?" The girl being asked did not understand what the teacher was saying. Also the girl did not know the English for what she wanted to express, and so began to cry as the only way to express what had happened to her.

"Why are you crying?" The teacher was worried. She kept asking for the reason but the girl only kept crying. Finally the teacher put her hand on the girl's shoulder and shook her repeating, "What happened?" in a loud voice. When I asked the girl for the reason she said, "I did not do anything wrong. I was beaten by a boy." In those days, both public school teachers and children seemed to have lots of worries.

After the ordeal of trying to comprehend the English of teachers in the public school was over, all the children went back to the Japanese school feeling relieved. They enjoyed coming to Japanese school and playing with friends there. It was really touching. As months and years successively followed, these children made very good grades at both the public and Japanese school. They became magnificent young people as they graduated. Now, seventy years later, I can remember those children clearly and deeply. In my mind there are so many dear memories.

The Japanese school being so very far from home, made it difficult for both parents and children. After several discussions they decided that these children would board at my home. Now my life style suddenly changed and became much busier. I woke up very early to prepare breakfast for them. First we all paid our respects to the Buddha, then we had breakfast. I made lunch for them to take to school. Before going to public school I gave them an hour of Japanese lessons. After sending the children to public school I cleaned the house, prepared for the afternoon lessons, and before long it was lunch time. In the meantime, the elementary children came home from Waiohinu public school. Every day was as though I were being overtaken by time.

After giving lessons for one hour to the elementary class and another hour to the advanced class in the afternoon, I did my laundry and then it was already time to prepare supper. I sent the children to their baths and after supper helped with their homework. After that was over we folded our hands in gassho to the Buddha and off they went to bed. Finally I had my own time. Well, this was really a short time, for right away someone may knock at the door saying, "Good evening." They had come to ask for help in writing a letter to their parents in Japan. Evenings I also had a class for young men. Morning, afternoon, and evening I was in full speed. I thought to myself that I worked hard and was really surprised about how I always seemed to accomplish my daily schedule. Especially when I had to write a letter home for someone, no matter how busy I was, I wrote without making any unpleasant face and did not forget to smile. When these people, who were not able to write a letter to their parents, brothers or sisters, asked me modestly with a few words to

14

write for them I felt that it must have been painful for them to ask and I simply did not have the heart to refuse. They were all happy and while in many cases I was not too useful to them, this letter-writing was one thing I knew I did well for them and I was glad.

Time passed and after a while the children who boarded with us again went to school from their homes. Thereafter, I thought I would have more time, but that lasted for just a brief interval. This time I was asked by a Pahala landowner to take girls in marriageable age at my home and I agreed to his request. These girls wanted to learn sewing and etiquette from me. Ever since I started to teach sewing during my free time from school, I had more time than when I was taking in children as boarders. In fact, since these girls helped me with cleaning and cooking in the morning and evening, my life became somewhat more relaxed. However, being in charge of marriageable-age girls, I felt that I had a great responsibility. At weddings in those days, most of the brides wore Japanese kimono of formal *"susomoyo montsuki,"* and *"maruobi."* Among these girls, three of them were able to sew their own wedding gowns.

Parents trusted us, so many important matters were left up to us which gave them relief. There was no safe or locker in my house, yet, many times people left their important documents such as bank deposit books with us. Sometimes, there were people who even left their deposit books and legal seal with us for half-a-year or more. Once a year the young men had to send a petition for draft deferment to the Japanese military department. If it was delayed and the period expired, they had to send a request for extension. However, working at distant mountains digging tunnels they could not come down just to ask us to send in their extension request. Therefore, they often left their legal seals with us for several

15

years. I think it cost about one dollar to register at the Japanese Consulate. Of course, I paid all in advance for them. The annual postponement was an established matter so we took the responsibility and submitted the requests to the Japanese Consulate. The young men completely relied on us to do so and felt free and at ease. Again during that time there were no mistakes or trouble. During my early missionary period, the minister and his wife were like social welfare workers, community workers, and performed various kinds of work one after another. The Nembutsu was alive in my daily life.

In this rural countryside, there was no doctor or licensed midwife. We lost our first son Johji right after birth. Since then, I oftentimes became ill. For three months I was in Honolulu for medical treatment and caused my husband much worry. The poverty and pressure of work must have caused him great distress and suffering. However, I have not heard even one complaint, or seen any unpleasant expressions on his face showing his difficulties. Thanks to the kindness of others, I recovered my health and later gave birth to our second son, Akira. However, my father in Japan, who had regretted my coming to Hawaii, had already passed away. Since I had no hope of showing my child to him, I was greatly saddened.

# Visiting Japan After Six Years

I HAD BEEN in Hawaii six years when I visited Japan on August 8, 1919, with my son Akira. He was eighteen months old. The purpose of my going back to Japan was to visit my father's grave and also to recuperate from my illness. Just before we boarded the ship, Akira was stricken with the flu. I was told that the ship was crowded with passengers from the mainland, and therefore, we were forced to accept berths in the third class in which a number of people were put together. On top of that, there was heavy rain and strong winds. The sea boiled in a great storm. Most of the passengers became seasick and were forced to stay in bed. Such were the circumstances. From a porthole, the sea water splashed over the bed. It was simply terrible.

Akira was a "father's child" and because of his high fever and loneliness he cried for his father. He clung to my arm and cried because he was afraid of the ship's doctor. Miss I., the ship's supervisor, kindly said, "Please come to my room because it is spacious and has a bed." Because she had a white uniform Akira was afraid of her. He thought she was a doctor. Finally through the courtesy of the ship's personnel, a bed for us was placed in the empty space at the exit to the dock. I used a flashlight throughout the night to get about. Gradually Akira

17

became well but caring for him took all my time and I had no time even to fix my hair. As we were leaving Honolulu Harbor, I was asked to accompany a young girl from the mainland who was on her way to visit her relatives in Japan. She said, "Please let me take care of your son." But she was also weak with sea-sickness. It was pitiful. My trip was a continuation of worries. At the end of the ten days' voyage, I was physically and spiritually exhausted. My anticipation of visiting Japan turned out to be, instead, a great suffering.

My mother and sisters came to Yokohama to meet me. At first sight they thought I was ill. Instead of my having come to visit my father's grave, they thought I came back because of my illness. Later this became a laughing matter. However, my mother thought I was suffering from tuberculosis and was secretly thinking of a place for my recuperation. That is how thin and emaciated I was. When I reached my parent's home at Aoyama, Akira was completely recovered from his flu. I also regained my strength, and I was very happy that I had returned home to Japan.

The flu that was raging all over the world also spread to Japan. Tokyo was in a panic-stricken condition. Every hospital was overcrowded with patients. Consequently doctors were so busy that they could not visit the patients at home.

Unfortunately, I was also stricken with the flu and suffered greatly. Being resigned to my death, I even left a verbal will about Akira. Fortunately, my younger sister was a doctor. She managed her working hours at the hospital so that she could visit me and check my condition every day. Because of this intensive care I was able to recover. I asked my mother to accompany me to my husband's parents' home in Saga. From Tokyo to Saga it took two nights on the train. Luckily Akira was now well but I was happy that my mother accompanied us to Saga. I stayed there about three months.

Everybody treated us so kindly that my son and I both recovered completely, mentally and physically. My thoughts were filled with gratitude and appreciation. As the days gradually approached for us to return to Hawaii, I felt reluctant to say farewell. My tears flowed.

After returning to Tokyo, cousin Jun and a relative, Sumio, became Akira's playmates. He spent happy days together with them. On the other side of the fence next door was the residence of Count Arima. When they heard that Akira was the same age as their son, a nurse escorted their son out of the gate to play pitch ball with Akira. They both looked very happy. This scene in my mind is as if it were just yesterday.

I left Akira in my mother's care while I prepared to return to Hawaii by making a trip around Kanda bookstores in search of reference books and games and craft books to use in Japanese school in Hawaii. During my stay in Tokyo we also went to Shinshu to visit my father's grave. This was the first time Akira saw snow in his life. He spent enjoyable days playing in the snow with his cousin. I regretted that I could not see my father's face. However, I was very happy seeing my healthy mother and relatives after such a long time. At Saga I was able to spend wonderful moments with them.

When I had left for Hawaii six years earlier, my three sisters were still students. Now, of the three, one was married, another had become a physician and the youngest sister was a teacher. Time passed quickly as we three sisters talked to each other and recalled our dear childhood days.

Finally, the morning for departure to Hawaii came. Everyone came aboard to see us off but the visitors had to leave a few minutes before departure time. When my mother and Akira's playmate cousins were about to leave the ship, Akira suddenly cried, "I am going to get off too." Until then he was quiet, but when he realized that he could not go down from the ship together with his new friends, he sadly shouted, "Obaa-chan! Jun-chan!" All during the ten days of our voyage to Hawaii he kept nagging me, saying, "I want to go back to Aoyama."

Sharing our cabin on the trip was a young lady by the name of Ibusuki-san, who was going to the mainland all by herself for the first time. She said that every time Akira cried saying, "Obaa-chan! Jun-chan!" she also cried because she wanted to go home, too. If she were not on the ocean, she would have wanted to return to Tokyo. Later Mrs. Watanabe of Sumitomo Shokin Ginko, who also boarded the ship with us at Yokohama, said, "When your son cried for 'Obaa-chan' I also wept in sympathy for him." When she told this to me, I came to think that I certainly caused a lot of trouble to others on this trip. I fully realized that one should avoid taking a young child on a trip and causing him such a painful experience.

# A Concern for the
# Japanese Language School

THERE WERE MANY organizations affiliated with the temple, such as Fujinkai, YBA, Sunday school and Japanese school. In spite of my busy schedule at the temple I was happy to participate in most of their activities. The eleventh session of the Territorial Legislature of both the House of Representatives and the Senate passed a law restricting foreign language schools. The Japanese language schools were particularly targeted, and after the governor of the territory signed this bill, regulations controlling the teacher's qualifications became very stringent. There were some teachers who could not qualify and had to leave, causing great hardships for us.

Within the Naalehu Hongwanji jurisdiction of Honuapo Japanese school and the Hiilea Japanese school, there was a total of less than thirty students each. The principals also served as teachers. Both of them resigned from their positions, which caused a crisis. Nobody wanted to work in such a troublesome and restricted situation, and besides no one wanted to become a teacher with such low salaries. Yet, school was important. We could not close the school. My husband was greatly worried and after much reflection he consulted with the parents as to his solution, to which they agreed. The solution was that I was sent to Honuapo and Mr. Masaru Murakawa was sent to Hiilea school. Because I was transferred to Honuapo from Naalehu school where I had been teaching, Naalehu asked for the temporary teacher.

The Sunday school schedules for Honuapo and Hiilea had changed to Saturday afternoon after Japanese school, creating much difficulty for our temple operation. For this reason Saturday became a very busy and painful day for me. On Saturday, I went to Honuapo school early in the morning and taught Japanese. After the lessons were over, I taught dharma class, and sang Buddhist gathas exactly as I had done on Sundays. When that was done I had to hurry on foot to Hiilea, and after that service was over, I hitched a ride on Murakawa Sensei's car to Naalehu. As soon as I reached home, I hastily had my lunch. From one to three o'clock I taught sewing, and after that was completed, I immediately started preparing supper, took in laundry, and did odds and ends working around the house. After supper, I went to Waiohinu, more than two miles away in order to take English lessons for the sake of the Japanese language school teacher's qualification examination. During that period my husband took me to and from school in his car. There were temple services and miscellaneous duties for my husband but I did not want to inconvenience the members and also it was not good for my three year old Akira to be left by himself, so I took him with me to school.

One Saturday, an incident happened. From Honuapo school to Hiilea school I was walking along an uneven rugged road under the hot sun, wiping off my perspiration. On one side of the road there was a wooded area and bushes above a cliff where the waves of the Pacific Ocean were dashing on to the rocks on shore. On the other side there was a lava field and pasture beyond which stretched a large canefield. Far off in the distance above the canefield, majestic, 13,000 feet high Mauna Loa. Not a sound was to be heard on this lonely road. Suddenly something arose in me that I could not contain. Uncontrollably, in a loud voice I called "Okaasan!" "Mother!". Large drops of tears kept rolling down my cheeks. Suddenly the nembutsu rose out of me: "Namu Amida Butsu!" I had just returned from my visit to Japan where I had seen my mother after an absence of six years. The memories of being with mother still lingered in my mind and my longing for her love made me call out "Okaasan." Even now writing this 60 years afterwards it seems as if it happened only yesterday. In retrospect, my husband probably had a more difficult life than I, and yet he did not complain.

# A Wedding Ceremony

WEDDINGS BECAME VERY numerous around 1913, when the children of the early immigrants to Hawaii reached marriageable age. In 1914, we were asked for the first time to serve as matchmakers and so we agreed. Thereafter, while we were residing in Naalehu, we acted as go-between for nearly seventy to eighty percent of the Japanese weddings in Naalehu. When I say this, it sounds as if we were meddling in these affairs, but the truth was that ninety-nine percent of them were already pre-arranged. We just added the crowning touch since match-makers were required by the prevailing custom. Such being the case we were most grateful.

In those days, the engagement gifts from the side of the bridegroom included a complete set of *"montsuki"* (garment with family crest) and *"maruobi"* (one piece sash, literally meaning 3 x 3 = 9) for the bride to wear on the wedding day, "sake," and fresh fish to which were attached the gold and silver strings called *"noshi."* From the bride's side, *"hakama"* and other articles were sent to the groom. In alter years, instead of an article such as *"hakama,"* monetary gifts became more popular. At the beginning, the monetary gift as an engagement present was often one hundred dollars. In place of sake and fish, an extra twenty-five dollars was the standard amount. Later, two hundred dollars became more common. Of course there were exceptions.

From the bride's side, the money for the *"hakama"* was commonly half of what the bride received from the bridegroom. The procedure for obtaining the marriage license was the same as the present. Besides this, they also performed the Japanese style *"san-san-kudo"* (three cups of varying sizes are used from which the *"sake"* is drunk in three sips). Besides instructing the bride and groom in the American style ceremony of the march into the temple, we also taught the proper technique in the serving of the sake in the *"san-san-kudo"* portion of the ceremony. To teach this, it was very difficult. But there was something even more difficult, and that was the preparation of the food which lasted one week straddling the wedding day. When the wedding day was set, the groom's family first gave a party and invited people who would be helping on that day. This is called the invitation for the helpers and at that time they decided the individual duties. After their working hours, the helpers prepared the ceremony site, gathered utensils, and prepared for the party. Among these helpers the person in charge of the cooking had the heaviest responsibility. Someone with cooking experience became the chairperson and women helped prepare the food in their own respective areas.

The main guests on that day were from the bride's side and the groom's family guests were only men. The following day only the women guests were invited. The cleaning up after the wedding and the party given to the hard working helpers extended the affair to seven days. The food committees were also in charge of food. It was a lively and cheerful series of affairs. There was no refrigerator in those days. Ice was packed into a large wooden box and large fish were placed in there ready to be used. When the large plate of maguro (bluefin tuna) sashimi was gone, a new plate always replaced it. This continued before and after the wedding, therefore, quite a few maguro had to be kept iced. We cannot even dream of such a spectacle these days when everything is so expensive, especially the fish. This scene of my bygone days vividly returned to my mind.

# World War I

WORLD WAR I broke out in 1914 and on August 29 of the same year, according to an alliance treaty with England, Japan declared war against Germany. The United States was still a neutral country. However, she sent munitions and many other materials to aid the side of the allied countries. The United States also vigorously aided the relief fund for refugees and for the care of orphans.

The United Sates declared war against Germany on April 6, 1917, and at the same time the United States enacted a law to draft soldiers. Immediately, young Japanese-American men volunteered. A company of Japanese-Americans was formed. Their record was good, and they were well received by the public.

The first Japanese that joined the army from our Ka'u district were thirteen boys from Naalehu and sixteen from Pahala. They were all members of our Hongwanji temple and YBA. The majority of them were young boys from Japan who could not speak English. When the time came for these young soldiers to be sent off to the front, people living in the Ka'u district came out in full force waving American flags to see them off as far as Honuapo Harbor. Because of the war, both the well-wishers and those who were being sent off shed tears, knowing that this might be their last time together.

One family sent three sons to the front. There was another case of a young soldier who had to leave his newlywed young bride of a month. In another case a mother let her only son go to the battle field. These boys boarded the ship "Kilauea" and stayed on deck for a long time. What I clearly remember to this day is the pitiful sight of these young volunteers who upon entering the service had to endure the tragedy and suffering caused by their lack of knowledge of basic English. They could not even distinguish the orders for "right face," or "left face."

The Japanese men who entered the United States Army were gathered from various districts. Mr. Ishida was the tallest of all and stood at the head of the line. He was from Naalehu. The shortest was Mr. Sato who was also from Naalehu, and he held up the end of the line. They were all wonderful young men. They all showed smiles on their faces as they left for the front.

During the war, the United States government set up a campaign for self-sufficiency and self-support. We took the first decisive step and joined this movement. Representing the Hawaii Honpa Hongwanji Kyodan, a small pamphlet was distributed to all the islands entitled, "The Problem of Self-sufficiency and Self-support." The Naalehu Hongwanji, the YBA and the Fujinkai members especially devoted themselves to this project in action and practice. The YBA borrowed land from the Plantation Company and utilized their time in growing potatoes everyday after working hours and even on Sundays and holidays. This program motivated individual families to start raising their own vegetables.

The Fujinkai cooperated with the Red Cross Chapter and helped roll bandages. Sunday school children became foster parents of individual Belgian orphans and sent milk money from their savings. I think the amount was three dollars a month.

The war ended before long and the young men came back in good spirits which made me very happy. After returning to the plantation, these boys studied English and upon examination they obtained American citizenship. They then organized a club with the idea of maintaining lasting friendships and requested my husband to name the club. He gladly accepted, giving them the name *"Hakujujikai,"* the White Cross Club. Because he named the club he became the founding father and on special occasions he always received invitations. In addition to the volunteer Nikkei soldiers, there were others who expressed their desire to join the club. This gathering has continued since then.

Today the volunteer soldiers of World War I are already past their eighties. Many are deceased. In World War II their sons also joined the army. The 100th Infantry Battalion and the 442nd Regimental Combat Team are well known. The Japanese-American volunteer soldiers and draftees who battled at the front are famous for demonstrating the true spirit of the Japanese-American citizen of the United States.

# More Trips To Japan

IN JUNE, 1927, my husband, the Reverend Chikyoku Kikuchi, my son Akira and myself joined the Honolulu YBA excursion tour to Japan. Coincidentally Princess Setsuko Matsudaira who was betrothed to Prince Chichibu of Japan, and her party were on the same boat on their way home from England. She was a very attractive princess. Several days after we departed from Honolulu Harbor, a ballroom dance party was held for the first class passengers. The YBA tour group received a special invitation and all the members happily attended the party. I remember this wonderful occasion as if it were just yesterday.

At Tokyo we were welcomed by people from the Sumitomo Bank, Nippon Yusen Kaisha, Hongwanji and many other affiliated organizations. The invitation from Baron and Baroness Furukawa, and from Mr. and Mrs. Takayuki Asano (Mr. Asano was principal of Seikei High School, Tokyo), all made a deep impression on me. Most of the tour members were Asano sensei's former students while he was the principal at the Japanese High School in Honolulu. They felt at ease and chatted as if they were at home.

The other day I turned to my old album and I felt very sad when I realized that Mrs. Kiyoko Imamura, who conducted the tour, Mr. Minoru Yasui, YBA executive secretary; Mr. Asano, the principal; and my husband, all were not living any more. Even the members who were young then are also deceased. I was deeply moved and my heart filled with pain.

Fifty years ago when there was no air transportation to Japan, and also no radio or television, first hand knowledge about Japan could be gained only by going there. On the YBA tour the young men and women born in Hawaii experienced their first glimpse of Japan and her culture, which inspired them. They gained very much from this tour. In later years, some of them became important citizens and outstanding leaders who have played active roles in Hawaii's society. Whenever I see them, we reminisce about those by-gone days.


Because of the Emperor's enthronement ceremony in 1928, the Kokumin Newspaper Company sponsored an All Japan Grammar School Children's Work Exhibition, including children's work from Japanese Language Schools. Before my departure to Japan, our Naalehu Japanese Language School also submitted twenty odd pieces of children's work. An exhibition was on display at Ueno while I was in Tokyo. The children who passed the examination had their names previously announced in the newspaper.

To my surprise, the name of Kayono Shirakawa of Naalehu Japanese Language School was on the honorable mention list. Reading it, I thought I was dreaming. On the opening day, I went with my younger sisters to the Ueno exhibition hall and there saw calligraphy, brush painting, compositions, sewing, needle work, and handicrafts on display. All of the pieces were outstanding works of art that attracted my attention. Some were collaborative work by classmates. In front of every display were people gathered around so I was not able to appreciate them fully. The special selection works were displayed in a glass case in a special room. Among many of the outstanding works there were still even more specially selected works.

Among these latter I spotted the one from the Naalehu Language School. It deeply moved me and my tears flowed. My sisters said *"Onee-san, Omedeto"* (Congratulations). Holding their hands, I could only say *"Arigato"* (Thank you). The composition that was specially recognized was entitled "Mission Fulfilled as a Japanese-American Citizen of the United States." After leaving the exhibition I immediately sent a telegram to my husband in Hawaii to share with him this happy occasion.

Besides the student from Naalehu, Miss Uenoyama from Olaa, Big Island, received an honorable mention. Her work was also on display in the special section. I do not recall whether there were compositions from the other islands in the exhibition. Although my time was limited, I went to the exhibition hall again the following day to examine the exhibits more closely. I want to show this exhibit to the children back in Hawaii, I thought. The following year on April 29, 1929, a prize-winning certificate of recognition was received from Prince Hirotaka Fushimi, honorary chairman of the event. The recipients were honored at a presentation ceremony in Hawaii. There was a congratulatory message from Bishop Yemyo Imamura and cordial wishes from many others.

In November of 1928, I was fortunate enough to be standing in front of the Imperial Palace at a designated area for the Japanese National Department of Education, to witness the Emperor and Empress proceeding from the palace to embark on their journey to Kyoto where the accession ceremony was to be held.

On this day with the help of a sensei from the Tokyo Normal School as our guide, three of us; the principal of Coconut Island Japanese School on the Big Island; Mr. Ogata, principal of Moiliili Japanese Language School, Honolulu; and myself were visiting the schools in the Tokyo area.

The evening paper reported that people from as far as Hokkaido and also from Taiwan came especially to Tokyo to witness this great spectacle. The news included an illustration of people spending the night on the cold roadside just for a chance to see the royal couple. The melody of *"Kimi Ga Yo"* (National Anthem) was clearly heard from within the palace grounds as the solemn and impressive procession moved from the Imperial Palace to the Tokyo Station.

# December 7, 1941

THE NIGHT BEFORE December 7, 1941, we honored the elders of the temple at a Bodhi Day celebration sponsored by the YBA members. Early the next morning, I sent my husband off to Hilo to attend the opening meeting of the education committee at Hilo Betsuin. While I was preparing for my Sunday school service, Mr. Hamada, the YBA president, dashed in and said, "Okusan, an awful thing has happened. There is a rumor that Japan has bombed Pearl Harbor." I was shocked and disbelievingly turned on the radio. Unmistakably an announcer was confirming that this terrible thing had occurred. The announcer went on to give details of the great confusion in Honolulu. As the innocent children came for Sunday school, I told them, "We will not have Sunday school service today; and you must go home." Shocked and fearful at hearing of the Pearl Harbor attack, many people came to the temple seeking advice.

My husband came home from Hilo in the afternoon. He said that they, too, were not aware of the incident at the morning meeting but just as they were about to have lunch, a message was received stating that war had broken out

34

between Japan and America and that everyone should return home immediately. This was shocking information. Panic-stricken, the ministers left Hilo with empty stomachs.

We were warned that lights were to be made invisible from our houses but every household was not prepared to handle this situation. Even when a tiny streak of light was seen, the soldiers from a guardpost came and issued warnings.

At midnight, someone knocked at the door. My husband got up to answer the knock and found a Hawaiian police officer friend standing at the door. "Rev. Kikuchi, I want you to come to the office for a minute." My husband left with him but soon after returned home. The policeman told him "I want you to go to Volcano and because it is cold there you should take some warm clothing. You may have to stay there two or three days." I borrowed the policeman's flashlight and in the darkness, gathered some warm clothing and put them into a bag. After changing his clothes, he picked up the "Shinshu Seiten" from the bookcase and put it into his pocket. As he left he said, "There is nothing to worry about, I will return in two or three days. But I want you to inform the resident Japanese that we are now in an unexpected situation. Because we are governed by the United States everyone must respect and obey the law of the government and continue to work earnestly. Whatever happens, be patient, control yourself, and never argue or fight with people of other ethnic groups. As for me, nothing to worry about because I have done nothing wrong. After this investigation is over, I will come home." Then he disappeared into the darkness with the officer.

Early the following morning, Mr. Beatty, the plantation boss, came and comforted me, saying, "Mrs. Kikuchi, the situation between the United States and Japan has become bad, but I think that Reverend Kikuchi will be coming home soon." After saying this, however, he requested that all of the

Japanese-American men, regardless of whether they were first or second generation, report to the Japanese language school at 2 o'clock that afternoon. I immediately telephoned those persons in charge of Waiohinu, Honuapo, and Hiilea, using the plantation boss's home phone.

The war had changed our friendly climate overnight. We were now considered enemies. It caused me great pain to face members from other ethnic groups. So with a heavy heart, I went again to the home of the plantation boss. His wife said, "Mrs. Kikuchi, war is between the United States and Japan; not you and me." Her compassionate words struck me and tears began to flow from my eyes. I humbly asked her to convey my message to the persons in charge of the Miss Taylor Camp, Puumakani, Waiubata, Kaalaiiki, and Ninole by telephone. This was done and that afternoon at 2 o'clock, all first and second generation Japanese-American boys gathered at the designated Japanese Language School building.

Mr. Beatty, the plantation boss said, "Gentlemen of Japanese ancestry, it is regrettable that war exists between the U.S. and Japan. Because we are living in America we must repect American law. I would like you to continue to work earnestly and peacefully. Never argue or fight with members of other ethnic groups."

"Both Reverend Kikuchi and Mr. Suzuki have been taken to Volcano Army camp," he continued, "but I think they will be coming home soon." After Mr. Beatty spoke, I humbly asked for an opportunity to convey my husband's message to the Japanese people of Naalehu. If this had been an ordinary day, several members would have remained after the meeting to socialize in our living room but today, everyone went home. I was there alone; thinking about what I should do, when I realized it was way past sunset, and the sky was dark.

As soon as the investigation was over, I had hoped that my husband would be home, but I waited a week, then two weeks, and yet he did not return. Perhaps by Christmas, I thought. Maybe by New Year's. My hopes and expectations were in vain. I received no word from him.

As an enemy alien, my bank savings account and my checking accounts were frozen, and I suffered a great deal.

The most difficult situation for me at the time was being unable to send funds for tuition to my son Akira who was studying on the mainland. One day, I received a letter from Akira which read, "I deeply regret that war has broken out between Japan and the United States. Father and Mother, you must be at an awful loss, but please try not to worry about me. I am always with the Buddha. Even if you are unable to send me money, I will work as a school boy and go to school." While I was relieved and happy at reading this letter, I was concerned about him. I knew he needed money to buy his winter clothing. While worrying about Akira, a second letter arrived. It read, "Mother, you have always written to your friends to ask them to look after me but now I am the one who is in the position to look after them, so please do not send such a letter."

During the way, Japanese-Americans on the mainland were evicted from their homes with only a single suitcase. This I learned later on. I also learned that Akira became a school boy right after the outbreak of war. When Akira learned that his father was transferred to the mainland, he brought his father his favorite past-time game, "go" which consisted of a board and stones, *"go-ban"* and *"go-ishi"*. During my husband's four years of internment, this game helped console him and his friends.

Later on we learned that in April of 1942 students such as Akira who were studying on the mainland were also assembled in camps. When grammar and high schools were started for the children interned there, Akira was employed as a teacher in the high school for which he received a small salary. Before long, interned individuals were allowed to volunteer for the Army. Akira volunteered but was not accepted because of a previous appendicitis operation. However, through a friend's intercession, he became an instructor of Japanese language at a military school for the duration of the war.

# Rumours and Martial Law

WHILE THE NUMBER of mainland soldiers increased in Ka'u the number of people who had been coming to the temple suddenly decreased. Only a few came now to the temple, and that was very seldom. Rumours somehow spread very quickly. "The F.B.I. came to search at Mr. Y.'s home and found a picture of Mr. Y.'s eldest brother, who lives in Japan, in a Japanese army uniform, therefore, he was taken to the F.B.I. office."

Another rumour was that one person was interned because a picture label of the Japanese flag was found on the cap of a bottle of medicine in his possession. There was another case where a policeman slapped an individual for speaking Japanese in the store. As such rumours spread, local Japanese became dreadfully frightened. I burned many of the precious books annd pictures I valued, except the religious books and text books. Some of the books were rare and price-less items we had collected over the years such as calligraphy of high priests, generals and officers of the navy, educators, and artists. A colleciton, bound into a three volume set, entitled "Senshin Ryoku," was burned.

Since my arrival in Hawaii, I had continued to keep diaries but now I burned these also. I burned the record books of names of donors who had contributed for the Kanto earthquake relief fund and for flood victims' relief fund. I later realized how foolish it was for me to do so, but at the time I was in a panic-stricken state. The local police supervisors were very strict and kept a close watch on us. While the temple was a gathering place for people before the war, no one would come anymore because of the fear of the F.B.I. It was only natural for them to feel this way, but it left me with an empty and sad feeling.

During the war, I completely lost interest in reading books, except religious ones. I put my heart, day and night, into reading Buddhist books. I realized that despite the circumstances, I must not forget "I am a Buddhist, and a Japanese woman, and not to take any action to dishonor this heritage."

One day, Mr. Sugai (Plantation Company secretary and Japanese school treasurer) visited me. "Yesterday, I was sent from the Plantation Company to interview internees about the management of their properties. I spoke with Kocho Sensei (Rev. Kikuchi) and he was very well. Sensei (addressing me) I have a message for you from Reverend Kikuchi. He said, 'Women of Japan have a tendency to be unnecessarily neglectful of their personal well being. Tell her to take good care of herself at all times.'" I was very surprised to hear that but to be honest, since the outbreak of the conflict, I was prepared to die if need be. I suddenly felt as though my husband had read my mind. When I went to Hilo earlier to do some shopping, I told our family physician that I am suffering from insomnia and that I wished to have some sleeping pills. And since it was not possible for me to come out to Hilo too often, I would appreciate it very much if he would let me have several extra pills, just in case I needed them. Of course I wanted to have the extra dosage in the event that I decided to take my life.

Immediately after the outbreak of war with Japan, martial law was established. As I wrote earlier, bank savings and checking accounts were all frozen. Gatherings of more than ten people were not permitted, and to go from Ka'u to Hilo, permission was necessary. The short wave radio was cut off. The Japanese newspaper was, of course, not available. Worst of all was the fact that my husband was interned and could not return home although at this time he was still in Hawaii. Such sad and painful days!

One day Mrs. Suzuki (her husband was also interned) came to see me saying, "My friend in Hilo tells me that tomorrow my husband will be going to the Hilo Court House. Reverend Kikuchi may be together with him so let's go to see them. I was told that the internees are at the Hilo Post Office compound, where the court house is located, everyday, so if we stand near the post office hallway probably we can see them pass, and at that time at least we can exchange a few words." Early the next morning Mrs. Suzuki and I went to Hilo. There were many people already standing along the post office hallway. Mrs. Suzuki and I also stood and waited. Presently a large army truck pulled up and a large number of internees climbed down from the truck. We knew most of them. We greeted them and inquired after their health, just said a few words to each other as they passed by. Mr. Suzuki stopped in front of me and said, "Okusan, Rev. Kikuchi's investigation was over a week ago. He is very well." I was very happy to hear that, but truly I would have wanted to see my husband even briefly. Even after that there was no one who was released to return home.

Akira was at that time as yet unaware of his father's internment. We wrote inquiring about Mr. Matsui, a Honolulu banker whom he knew very well. "Wasn't Mr. Matsui interned and transferred to the mainland?" he asked. Transferring internees from Hawaii to the mainland was unbelievable, I thought at first, but later I was rudely awakened to the realization of my ignorance concerning the situation we were facing then.

Occasionally I visited Mrs. Tamekuni from Pahala Hongwanji and Mrs. Mochizuki of Kapapala Nichiren-shu. We would spend a night sympathizing with, and comforting each other. However, due to the distance of thirteen and seventeen miles separating us, we seldom had the opportunity to do that.

# The Internees

IN THIS WAY the new year of 1942 passed. One day in February, an unexpected news was released saying, the internees will be allowed to see their families. The members of the families were very excited and happy and began preparing favorite foods day and night, for their fathers, husbands or brothers. On that day there were people who had left their homes before dawn with carloads of children to travel a hundred miles to visit their loved ones. As usual I had a ride with Mrs. Suzuki's family. As I got down from the car and walked together with a large crowd across a spacious area, a building surrounded by wire mesh fence became visible. As I approached closer to the wire-fence, I could see the internees' faces fastened to the fence as they eagerly awaited the arrival of their family members. "Mrs. Kikuchi, sensei is here," I heard a voice. After three months of insecurity and a feeling of uneasiness due to our separation, we were finally allowed to see each other. Holding each other's hands there was no word necessary to express the joy of reunion.

Through the kindness of the officer-in-charge, the internees' families were relaxed and they spread out their homemade lunch on the lawn and enjoyed eating, chatting, and laughing. There was no end to their conversation. The MP's showed no sign of concern in the families' conversations and furthermore they even over-looked the time limit in the visiting hours. They were very generous and friendly. The first thing I handed out to my husband was a letter that I brought with me from Akira. For my husband, that letter from his son was his greatest concern. In this letter Akira says, "I am always with Buddha so please do not worry about me. Although you do not send me money I'll work as a school boy and study." Reading Akira's letter my husband was relieved and extremely happy.

Finally, the time of departure arrived. Volcano towards the evening is rather chilly. We do not know when we will be able to meet again. Perhaps this might be the last time! Those remaining, those leaving, both said reluctant farewells to each other. There was a scene where a little child waved his hand crying, "Daddy bye-bye." There were other scenes of mothers or wives, with tears in their eyes, waving their hands, loathing to part. I can still see these scenes vividly before my mind's eye. This moment of farewell was very, very sad indeed.


It was not long after this visit that the families were informed the internees were being transferred to the mainland. The internee families were shocked and saddened. They had only two days in which to prepare and deliver to the internees winter clothing. Since winter clothing is not normally necessary in Hawaii we had a great difficulty locating such clothing. I, too, left for Hilo on a scheduled taxi early the following morning after the announcement to look for appropriate clothing but clothing shops in Hilo normally did not have any necessity to stock up in warm clothing. Even materials to make such warm clothing had been sold out. I was finally able to locate something that would serve the purpose but only after visiting several clothing and dry goods stores, causing me to miss the last scheduled taxi returning to Naalehu.

The winter clothing materials that I purchased had to be sewn that evening and his name embroidered and delivered in the morning but I had no way of going home. With such confused feelings, I had not a moment to cry. Looking at the approaching gloomy skies, I wondered what I should do. If this were ordinary times I could have gone to my many friends and acquaintances in Hilo for help but in the present situation the internee's families could not be too friendly and had to refrain from going to their homes. I was standing by the roadside, my head filled with such a complicated feeling when a car suddenly stopped in front of me. I heard someone calling, "Mrs. Kikuchi, I was looking for you, hurry and get in this car," and he carried my packages. He was Mr. Tadasuke Nakabayashi. "Buddha in hell" must be in this kind of a situation. I put my hands together in gassho and thanked him. Forty years have passed, and now as I write of this incident tears of gratitude flow onto my paper. Mr. Nakabayashi told me that Mrs. Shiba, a minister's wife, saw me late in the afternoon shopping and so he reasoned that since I had no way of going back to Naalehu I must surely be in trouble. He had gone around the city two or three times to finally locate me. I truly had no other way to express my gratitude for his kindness but to fold my hands in gassho.


As soon as I reached Mr. Nakabayashi's home, Mrs. Nakabayashi welcomed me very warmly. Mrs. Shiba was also there. Mrs. Shiba's husband, as in my case, was also interned and she was also in Hilo to buy winter clothing for her husband. After we had eaten the warm-hearted supper she prepared for us, Mrs. Nakabayashi helped Mrs. Shiba and me with our sewing. When we were finally finished with this task and were fully relaxed, there came a telephone call from Hilo Hongwanji for me. The caller said that he had received a call from Naalehu Hongwanji asking whether he knew my whereabouts, and that he was happy to have found me at Nakabayashi's. The message was a confirmation that Hiroshi Shirakawa of Waiohinu, who was on a military troop ship, was killed when the ship was sunk. The funeral service were to be held on the following day. I was to return to Naalehu with Rev. Kanda of Hilo Betsuin, who would be conducting the funeral services. It was, indeed, a very sad news, this unexpected telephone call.

Hiroshi Shirakawa was the beloved son of Mr. and Mrs. Hayato Shirakawa. He had graduated with honors from both the Naalehu Public School and the Japanese School. After graduating from both elementary schools he went on to Hilo and graduated from Hilo High School and from Hilo Hongwanji Japanese High School. He was working at the Naalehu Plantation store when he was drafted and sent to war. My relationship with Hiroshi started from his birth. While an infant his mother used to carry him to the temple services and to the Sunday school services and did not miss a single Sunday. During the eight years as my Japanese school student, he was a good friend of my only son Akira. Hiroshi was an intelligent and cheerful boy and was loved by everyone. The night before he entered the army I was invited to his send-off party. The scene of that party still appears before my mind's eye as if it were a dream. The relationship between Hiroshi and the Nakabayashi family was also close. We were all so suddenly saddened, we folded our hands in gassho and said the nembutsu together.

All the articles that were to be sent to my husband the next day were ready so I went to bed but could not sleep.

Next day I was accompanied by Rev. Kanda of Hilo Hongwanji to Naalehu. On my way home to Naalehu we stopped at the Volcano Army Camp. I delivered my husband's warm clothing and conveyed the incident of Hiroshi. My husband was so surprised, and with a sorrowful face said, "What a pitiful thing to have happened!" With tears in his eyes he recited the nembutsu, and said, "Please express my deepest sympathy to his parents."

When I would meet my husband again was very unpredictable, but I was not permitted to stay too long. I said my last farewell holding his hand and I hurried back to Naalehu. Right away I changed my clothes and together with Rev. Kanda I went to Waiohinu where the Shirakawa family lived.

Hiroshi Shirakawa was the first Naalehu boy who died as an American soldier. In spite of his honorable death the funeral was very simple, attended only by the people of Waiohinu and the Japanese living in Naalehu. No one came from the Army Intelligence Department or from the plantation store where he had been employed. Although it was immediately after the outbreak of war and martial law was in effect, I felt very said that it could not have been otherwise.

The investigations of the internees were very strict. The individual records were minutely recorded at Hilo Court, and were compiled in detail. For instance the authorities would say, "You gave a speech at such and such a place on a certain month and day," or "You gave to Japan a certain amount of donation," etc. Even the person in question did not remember his past deeds, but the FBI had such complete files on their personal histories that not one of them could say a word. However, none of them had a guilty conscience, therefore, in that respect they were not afraid.

In the case of my husband, there was no heavy interrogation. He was simply asked, "How is your body condition?" or "How about the food?", and the questioning was more like light conversation. When people heard this, they started saying Reverend Kikuchi is old so he will be released soon. However, he was among the first sixteen persons from the Big Island to be shipped off to the mainland.

The boat Hiroshi Shirakawa was on as previously mentioned, was going to drop off the soldiers in Hilo and later pick up the sixteen internees, including my husband, and go to Honolulu to join the other internees there. They were to be the first internees to be sent to the mainland but that boat was sunk by a Japanese torpedo. Therefore, the first internees were delayed in their departure. I learned all this later.


When their families heard that the internees were being transferred from the Volcano Army Camp on that day to the mainland, they came to stand from early morning along the road from Volcano Army Camp to send them off. Before long, one, two, three trucks with canvas covers fastened sped by carrying the internees. Because of the canvas covering of the trucks, only those few seated at the rear end could be seen. But we waved our hands with all our might, raised our voices "Take good care of your health and please do not worry about us," and sent them off.

Soon after, a notice was sent to the families stating, "If the families desire to transfer to the mainland and wish to live together with husbands, parents, or with brothers, you will be granted the privilege to do so." It was a notification from the Army. At that time practically all the island ministers' wives and their families moved to the mainland, but I had a question in mind. "If this is the Army's order to go, then I will go, but if this is a choice, then I shall remain here," I replied.

Mrs. Tamekuni from Pahala Hongwanji, Mrs. Mochizuki from Kapapala Nichiren-shu, and Mrs. Matsuura of Kona Hongwanji all left the island and moved to the mainland. Since we had occasionally been seeing and comforting each other, after they moved to the mainland I suddenly became lonely. On the island of Hawaii the Rev. Zenei Aoki of Hilo Hongwanji Betsuin was the only remaining minister. Of course, ministers of other sects were also interned.

# Destruction of Pahala Hongwanji Temple by Fire

IN THE EARLY morning of January 18, 1943, I received a telephone call from a person in charge of the temple saying, "Pahala Hongwanji main worship hall, Japanese language school and also the teacher's residence were completely burnt down this morning. The cause of the fire is unknown." I was surprised and startled. I wanted to go to Pahala right away but I could not. I waited till the following day. (During the war the internees' families were very timid about doing things.) When I reached Pahala that next day I just stood there blankly gazing at the terrible ashen remains of the once beautiful Japanese style main worship hall, the language school, and the teacher's residence.

Incidentally, the main worship hall, which was built in 1903, had been the oldest Japanese style temple on the Island of Hawaii and boasted the most magnificent altar.

The school building had been a large two-storied structure, of a type seldom seen at that time in the islands. It was equipped with the latest convenience and facilities, and had just been completed with great pains and labor by Rev. Tamekuni and the temple members and school parents.

The teacher's residence, similarly, had just been completed together with the school building.

Because the fire broke out during the day time, fortunately the Buddha statue and the altar accessories were all carried to safety by the members. The Shingon-shu temple next door agreed to house the image of Amida Buddha.

Upon seeing the figure of Amida Buddha safely housed in the Shingon-shu temple Taishi-do next door, I folded my hands in gassho, tears rolling down my cheek. One by one people came to describe to me the scene of the fire. According to the account the first fire broke out in the school building, which was occupied by the military.

The people who gathered to watch the fire together with the Caucasian soldiers who were there suggested that the school building which was aflame should be destroyed in order to keep the fire from spreading to the temple. For some unknown reason the plantation manager failed to heed that suggestion. The temple, which might have been saved, also burned to the ground.

At that time the members of the Fujinkai surrounded me. One of the members, Mrs. Toguchi, said, "Mrs. Kikuchi, please do not go to the mainland," and her eyes were filled with tears. Other Fujinkai members also joined in, saying "Please do not go, we are all depending on you." It surprised me to know that the members trusted and relied upon even such a person as myself. "I'll not go to the mainland unless it is an order from the military," I said. "We're all together with the Buddha. Let us help each other," they replied. Because the members trusted and depended on me, I made a firm decision to stay on and vowed to work and help as much as I could.

# Wartime in Naalehu

BEFORE THE OUTBREAK of World War II, there were several places in Hawaii that offered lessons in first aid treatment. At Naalehu a haole doctor from the plantation came and gave lectures every week. The public school teachers and also the young people of various ethnic groups registered for this course. I also took the course. Since I have contact with Japanese school pupils everyday, I cannot predict when the pupils will be injured or become ill, so I felt the necessity of learning such skills. Of course I never dreamed or expected that the war would break out. Bandaging, or carrying wounded people when actually seen with one's eyes can be understood, but the textbooks were in English. Learning by having them translated was more difficult than I thought.

One day, the doctor said, "After the lessons are over, I'll give you a test and present you with a certificate." Upon hearing this, four or five Japanese women who did not have confidence in their English ability suddenly stopped coming to class. I also wondered what I should do, but I didn't want others to think that I quit because I was afraid to take the test. So, one day I told the doctor, "If you let me take the test in Japanese I have confidence that I will receive an "A" but if it is in English, then I have no confidence." When I said this to the doctor, he laughed and said, "Please continue with your lessons. I'll give a test especially for you through an interpreter."

Because of his kindness I was able to receive a certificate along with the haoles and the other young people. Upon receiving the certificate we practiced at the park with mock wounded persons lying on the ground. Following the instructions pinned on the body we would give first aid and load them on a vehicle to have them taken to the hospital. Those of us with first-aid certificates were assisted by two young male attendants. Because I had received that sort of training, even after the war broke out I was able to help without feeling any discrimination.

But not everything went easily. One day, all of a sudden, I was called by the plantation boss. I was wondering what it was all about, when he said, "Mrs. Kikuchi, when you send a letter to your husband, the Rev. Kikuchi, do not write long letters in detail." I had forgotten that all letters were censored and I forgot that I was an enemy alien. My only concern was about my husband that he might be worried, so to make him happy I wrote long letters. It was my shallowness of thought and I was very ashamed of myself.


None of the Japanese were guilty of sabotage. They did not quarrel or violate the regulations. Everybody hoped that the war would end soon. During this critical time there were houses searched. People were called in to be questioned. Even if they searched my house I did not worry because I did not have a bad conscience. Most of my important papers that could have caused others problems were destroyed but no one came to search my house.

One day two young FBI investigators came and said in a rather haughty manner that they wanted to check on my school text book. They tried to take with them the stack of typing paper on the shelf that was bought for school use. I said, "That is not my personal thing. It has not been used yet, so if you want to take it with you, I will have to first consult Mr. Sugai, who is the school treasurer. He is at the plantation office. If he gives permission, then you may take it with you." Without any hesitation they said, "All right," and packed it in their automobile and left.

I was worried, so that evening I called Mr. Sugai on the telephone and related the incident. He said, "No one has come." He immediately reported what had happened to the plantation manager. The manager was extremely angry and he called the Hilo FBI office and reported to the person in charge. The next day the ream of paper that these two young men took with them was returned. The men then went to Mr. Sugai's office and said, "Mrs. Kikuchi said 'OK,' so we took the paper home. But she must have regretted her decision later." However, their conscience may have bothered them because thereafter, whenever we met they would talk to me first from their side. Their attitude had completely changed.

One day, a First Lieutenant of the United States Navy accompanied by Miss Higuchi as interpreter came and asked me if I have Japanese Language School books of such and such texts. If so, he wanted to borrow them. I said, "If there are any books you want please take them with you." and I led him to the bookshelf. Before long, the First Lieutenant took about ten books in his hand. At the entrance he called to me and through the interpreter said, "Today I am awfully sorry to intrude upon you, please pardon me. The books that I borrowed will be returned to you within a week." Compared to the previous two ill-mannered young FBIs, the First Lieutenant indeed was different, and worthy of being admired.

One day when I went to the *hondo* to change the water for the flowers, there was an envelope on top of the altar. I wondered who could it be from. On another day, another offertory envelope was left on the altar. Neither envelope had a name on it, so I was concerned. Then one morning, when another offertory envelope was placed on the altar, I saw Mrs. R. M. going down the *hondo* steps. And again, on another day, another offertory envelope had been placed on the altar. This time I saw Mrs. M. open the *hondo* door and saw her going into the worship room.

Worrying about my income being cut-off, these two persons were surreptitiously bringing contributions for me. I shed tears of joy when I discovered their kindness. Even though through our treasurer, Mr. Sugai, I was receiving from the headquarters a small amount for living expense, just as we had been before the war, I was still moved. In the case of Mr. M, he kindly said, "Mrs. Kikuchi, please come to my home when you are short of food. We can share whatever we raise in our garden."

Again, it happened one day, when Miss I. and Miss T. were on their way home from their work, they each gave me an orange they had received at their working place. "Sensei, today at our store there was a new shipment of oranges, however, just a box of oranges cannot be sold according to the shopkeeper and he divided the oranges among the employees. This is just one, but please accept it." I thanked them sincerely. Since the outbreak of the war, practically all oranges that came from the mainland went to the military. We civilians could hardly obtain them, so when I received these oranges I was quite overjoyed. In gratitude I offered the oranges first to the Buddha and then ate them.

The following day Mr. A. came, saying, "Sensei, the other day our store had a new shipment of oranges, but there was only one box, so the manager said, 'instead of selling them I will share them with the employees.' When I took it home my mother said, *'Otera-no-okusan* loves oranges, so although it is just one orange, she will appreciate it. Take it to her.' So I brought it. Sensei, it is only one orange but please accept it." He presented a delicious looking orange to me. I know at Mr. A.'s house, there are several small children who need nourishment more than I do, but he gave it to me. I was overwhelmed by their kindness. Many years have passed, yet, thinking of these oranges and the thoughtfulness of the donors, tears fill my eyes.

Mrs. Lowry, a public school teacher who taught me English at the time I took an examination for Japanese language school, frequently took me out to lunch. Mr. and Mrs. Kokubun sent their precious daughter to my place since I was living all by myself and let her spend every night at the temple. Many people kept their distance from the internee's families, but Mr. and Mrs. Kokobun's attitude were different. These thoughts are deeply engraved in my heart.

Again, the following happened. All of a sudden one day Mr. Sugai, the Japanese school treasurer, came and said, "Okusan, the military wants to use the school building as a commissary so I decided to lend them the building." I could only say, "Is that so?" for that was the only answer I could offer.

The school building was in the same location where I lived. At nights I could see the lighted cigarettes of the men smoking on the school lanai in the dark. I sensed the danger of fire but I could not go and tell them not to smoke. From then on there were many unfamiliar soldiers from the mainland who were going in and out of the premises throughout the day and night. That caused me much worry. I thought of moving out from here, and every time I saw heavily loaded trucks being unloaded at the facility, my worries became deeper and deeper. Presently, the captain of this commissary came to see me saying, "Mrs. Kikuchi, from today we will be using the school building. I am Capt. Chung, in command here. If you have any trouble please don't hesitate to tell me. Again, if you need to use the telephone, please do so anytime." He spoke to me in warm tones. I learned after a while that Mr. Chung had been a public school teacher before entering the Army.

Again, I was truly grateful for the kindness of this warm gentleman.


In the early period of the war sendoff parties for draftees and for the volunteer soldiers were not permitted.

Later, sendoff parties for the inductees were held at the clubhouse attended by the entire community. The nisei volunteers outnumbered the non-nisei volunteers by a large percentage. At every sendoff party I was asked to give the sendoff speech and inevitably I was compelled to get up and speak. The volunteers who sat at the table with their parents were mostly nisei, only 17 or 18 years of age. They were all my students who were until recently sitting at their classroom desks with their boyish faces.

Of these boys who are going to the war front, how many of them will return safely, I wondered. My heart was filled with apprehension and sadness, but I had to suppress such feelings to deliver the sendoff speech. And when the sendoff party was over I would go home and in the privacy of my room weep loudly.

The following morning at the sendoff I told each young man, "The Buddha is always with you," and gave them a Buddhist rosary, but whatever "nenju" I had at hand soon were all gone. I could only grasp the hands of the remaining boys and say, "The Buddha is always with you no matter when or where. When you are lonely or when you're in trouble, repeat 'Namu Amida Butsu.' Even if you cannot repeat His name, He will always be with you, so don't worry." Because they were all regular Sunday School pupils, they readily understood what I was saying. I was happy.

These young men had been taught over and over at the Japanese language school that it was important that America and Japan endeavor to deepen their mutual understanding of each other so that friendship and good will could be established. It was for that purpose that they, the children, were studying the Japanese language. Each young man, therefore, must have embraced within his heart a strong conviction of his duty as an American soldier.

As expected, the Japanese American units of the 100th Battalion, the 442nd Regiment and the Military Intelligence Service all distinguished themselves as outstanding units of the United States Army. When the first anniversary of the formation of the 442nd Regimental Combat Team was observed, Colonel Pence, after congratulating the unit's achievements and expressing gratitude for the men's effort and support, concluded by declaring, "I am extremely proud of the fact that I am your Commander!"


At first the Volunteers were billeted at Schofield Barracks for a period of basic military training. During that time the men were permitted to leave camp on Sundays to attend the temple or church of their choice. Most of the men from the neighbor islands attended Wahiawa Hongwanji which was located a few miles from Schofield Barracks. After listening to the Dharma talk the soldiers were treated to a delicious meal, lovingly prepared by the Fujinkai ladies.

Through letters received from these young soldiers who would soon be departing for the war front, neighbor islanders learned about the extreme kindness of the members of Wahiawa Hongwanji and were deeply moved and overcome with gratitude.

When the Naalehu Hongwanji members heard this beautiful episode they were all filled with admiration and gratitude. "Let us also help," thought the Naalehu Hongwanji Fujinkai, and immediately sent a small token of appreciation to Wahiawa Hongwanji with a note, "Please add this to your project."

For me, this is truly a heartwarming recollection.

# Re-opening Dharma Classes

IMMEDIATELY AFTER THE outbreak of the war the attitude towards the Japanese-Americans was one of skepticism. Harsh measures were taken against them, but among the internees there was no one who lacked integrity and among all Japanese-Americans there was not one single case of sabotage. Moreover, with almost all eligible Japanese-Americans responding to the call for volunteers, much of the suspicions of the community had been allayed. Permission was granted to reopen the Hongwanji Sunday School, which was closed when hostilities began. Several young men from Honohina hurried to bring in the good news. The great joy experienced when the students and I once again assembled before the altar of the Buddha to sing His praises will never be forgotten. As we sang tears trickled down my cheeks.

So my joyful and busy life began once again. Because it was necessary to enlist the cooperation of people to serve as teachers and helpers in order to reopen the Sunday Schools in Pahala and Kapapala, we drive around in Mr. Miyahata's car visiting people for many days, until we received the agreement from President Hashimoto of Pahala and Mr. Kai and Mr. Shintaku of Kapapala to look for Sunday School teachers.

Fortunately we were able to receive the backing of our Sunday School from such community leaders as the bank manager, plantation surveyor, public school teacher, office workers, and company department head. At Pahala there were Mr. Otsuka, Mr. Obayashi, Mr. Ezaki, Mr. and Mrs. Sato, Miss Kitagawa, Miss Saito, and Miss Furumoto; at Kapapala there were Mr. Nakashima and Miss Mizuno; and at Naalehu there were Mr. Tsugawa, Mr. Fujimoto, Mrs. Shimizu and Miss Taise, all of whom accepted our request. I visited these three places in turn, and held the highest esteem and much gratitude for these teachers who gave up their only day off during the week to volunteer as dharma school teachers.

Since both the Pahala temple and school had been lost to the fire we asked Mr. Cushnie, the plantation manager, if a plantation building could be used. Regrettably his answer was, "There is no need to have two Sunday Schools. The Christian Sunday school should be enough." Soon after, while he was directing the extinguishing of a cane field fire, Mr. Cushnie was unfortunately burned to death. He was succeeded by Mr. Ramsay, a person of culture, who soon was regarded by the workers as a kind father, and gained the trust of all. Upon his arrival Mr. Ramsay loaned the clubhouse to the Hongwanji, thus finally making it possible for Sunday School, religious services, and all other activities to be held in Pahala. My work now became doubly busy. Monthly services were held in six locations: Naalehu, Waiohinu, Honuapo, Pahala, Manya, and Kapapala. These involved family memorial services, funerals, and in addition there were trips to Hilo, Kona, and at times, the Honohina area.

Rev. Aoki (later Bishop Aoki) was extremely busy because he had to serve not only Hilo Betsuin, but also the temples in the outlying plantations, from which all Buddhist ministers had been interned. He requested, however, that all members who needed his services come to the temple, and of necessity curtailed all home visits.

During these difficult years, the assistance of the Sunday school teachers and organists was all the more appreciated. The following is a list of those who were most helpful:

From Naalehu: Tadayuki Tsugawa, Michio Fujimoto, Hiroko Taise, Hinako Ezuka, Emiko Fujita, Fujie Kobatake, Yoshie Obayashi and Katsuyo Koike. From Pahala: Atae Otsuka, Tsuneo Obayashi, Wataru Ezaki, Harue Furumoto, Tsukio Saito, Ethel Kitagawa, Ayako Iida, and Ms. Fukumoto. From Kapapala: Howard Nakashima, Mr. Mizuno, Mr. Kai and others.


Rumours during the war years, whether caused by mishearing, curiosity or evil intent, were the source of much confusion. There were persons who suffered a great deal because someone made up a story which was believed by the people. Once, in the case of a young lady, a rumor about her which was groundless began to spread, and in spite of the efforts of her close friends to counter the flow by citing the real evidence, an atmosphere of doubt continued to hang over her, causing her much grief.

In my case the incident ended as a laughing matter. One day I went out to Hilo to take care of some business and dropped by at Rimban Aoki's home. I was quite surprised when the Rimban and Mrs. Aoki welcomed me unusually warmly. Even their son seemed happy to see me. I always received their kindness but today I felt something different. Then the Rimban said, "Okusan, about 4 ot 5 days ago a woman came and said, 'I hear Mrs. Kikuchi of Naalehu has finally gone out of her mind. No one knows her where-abouts.' At first I didn't believe it. If it were true that you were missing I would have been informed by someone from Naalehu Hongwanji. But just a while ago another person came to say the same thing and I began to worry. Just now my wife and I talked about calling Naalehu when you appeared. That's why you must have thought how strangely we were behaving. Now that we know the rumour is not true, stay two or three days and take it easy!" So saying, we all had a good laugh.

Of the many rumours that appeared during the war one had to do with the "great vistory of Japan." This rumour spread widely, from the mainland to Brazil, but as most people know, only very few persons believed it. Rumours are trouble-som because the originator of the tale cannot be identified. It is an evil act to spread malicious rumours. During the war I graphically experienced the dreadfulness of rumours that may even cause someone's death.

# Casualties

ALL LETTERS DURING the war had to be written in Engligh, and letters by enemy aliens were, of course, censored. Those who suffered the most were Issei from Japan who could not read or write English. It was the greatest sadness that such people could not correspond with their sons overseas. I had a son on the mainland attending school and didn't know when he would be inducted in the service. It was difficult enough for me not to be able to write him, but for the boys overseas and their parents who could not communicate with each other, it was indeed an unbearable situation.

Because of this I decided to learn English from a public school teacher. With my newly gained skill I wrote short letters to all the nisei soldiers from the Ka'u district. Because of the war I'm sure not all the letters reached their destination, but those who received the letters wrote back saying how glad they were to be remembered. Young Tachibana wrote, "I was both surprised and happy to receive your letter . . . If only my mother could write English like you, how happy I would be."

Young Furusho's letter contained a snapshot of himself. "Today I went fishing with my friend at -------. If I return home

64

safely, I have lots of stories to tell you. . . ." But this young Furusho was killed in action. His smiling face still appears before my mind's eye.

"Sgt. James Tetsuo Higashi of 442nd Infantry Regiment was killed in action on the Italian front on July 12, 1944," read the casualty notice received by Mr. and Mrs. Yoshitoshi Higashi from the War Department. I was asked by the Higashi family to officiate at the memorial service. Rev. Ernest Hunt, who happened to be visiting from Honolulu, and I went to the home, chanted the Shoshinge and recited the Epistle by Rennyo Shonin. I asked Rev. Hunt to present the English Dharma-talk.

The photo of Sgt. James Tatsuo Higashi in Army uniform seemed as if he was talking to me, and my heart was filled with sadness. No matter how honorably he had died in combat, to the Higashi family he was a precious irreplaceable son. Understanding the pain being experienced by Mr. and Mrs. Higashi I had no words to assuage their sorrow. While he was a student at the University of Hawaii, he volunteered with his friend for the 442nd Combat Team and went to war as a Sergeant. On the Italian battlefront he was killed in action. Unlike HIroshi Shirakawa, who died immediately after the out-break of the war, Sgt. Higashi's funeral was according to Army regulations. High officials, the Army Band, the elite of Ka'u district, residents and various representatives attended the funeral rites. The main hall (hondo) was filled and more than half of the people gathered had to stand outside the hall.

This was the first time that a funeral for an American war casualty was held together with the military in Naalehu Hongwanji. Besides the military music on the program, I added a Buddhist gatha to be sung by the choir and conducted a very solemn ceremony.

For the four years of the war I did all of the funerals in the Ka'u district. Ordinarily a very timid person, I eventually had to go through the war all alone in Hawaii. In retrospect I am happy that my remaining in Hawaii alone was, indeed, not in vain. At the same time I am also grateful to my broad-minded husband and my son Akira. The joyful as well as difficult days I spent with all the temple members are today dear remembrances.

# My Husband Returns

IN GOING TO monthly services at Pahala and Kapapala, I reserved the only taxi in Naalehu, so I had no trouble going to those places. However, in travelling to other districts, I know I caused extraordinary inconvenience for Mr. Yoshiaki Miyahara and Mr. Isakichi Hashimoto, president of Pahala Hongwanji. When Mr. Miyahara and Mr. Hashimoto were busy, then I had to trouble other persons. One day Mr. Nanbu of Kapapala said, "Okusan, we will buy a car for you so will you please drive yourself?" To ride in a car for ten miles on the same road four times a day takes a lot of time, and I felt bad about asking people to drive me. But when I first started to drive I had a mishap and barely escaped death. After this bitter experience I completely gave up driving until my husband returned from the mainland. To ask people to take me back and forth from home was difficcult and I felt very bad about it, but I could not bring myself to drive at that time. Even now when I think of those who helped me with wartime transportation, I feel very grateful for their kindness.

During the war, my husband was sent to the mainland internee camp. He was gone for four years, but returned safely back home to Hawaii on November 13, 1945. The ship entered the Honolulu harbor at 2:30 pm. The following day I went to Hilo harbor with persons in charge of Naalehu Hongwanji to meet my husband. Seeing my husband at first glimpse, I was surprised at seeing him so thin, but he had a happy smile on his face and he exchanged greetings in high spirits. I was relieved. I took a deep breath. How grateful I felt to see him once again. We paid homage together at Hilo Betsuin then, at Hilo Inn, twenty to thirty people welcomed us. Mr. Shirakawa, Mr. Hamada, Mr. Fujioka, Mr. Takaki, and Mr. Miyahara were together in one car. As we approached Pahala, members of the temple turned out to welcome my husband who had returned after four years of absence. As soon as we arrived there my husband kneeled down in front of the temporary altar of Amida Buddha, reciting nembutsu as he shed his tears.

He stood stupefied for a while gazing sadly at the burnt remains of the temple, the school building and teacher's dwelling. Naalehu is thirteen miles beyond Pahala but some people from Naalehu came all the way to Pahala to meet and welcome him. Others stayed back to clean and beautify the temple. Still others made delicious food. In Naalehu my husband shook everyone's hand with great joy. Immediately they entered the *hondo* and at long last, after four years absence, recited the Shoshinge together. So many thoughts came to my mind and my tears rolled down my cheeks. Since then forty years have passed but it seems as if the reunion just happened yesterday as the scene appears vividly in my mind's eye.

After the four years of absence, there were many urgent matters waiting for my husband that had to be accomplished right away. Among them were the reopening of the Japanese Language School and the rebuilding of the Pahala Hongwanji Temple. This had to be rushed by all means. During the war, Naalehu Japanese language school had been taken over by the Army, therefore, the minister's residence was used as the classroom. Because no school building remained in Pahala the minister's home had to be used as a classroom when we reopened our Japanese Lanaguage School in 1946.

Compared to the enrollment before the war, the attendance of pupils was very small. With such minimal income, a teacher could not be hired, and so only my husband and I taught them. Since the outbreak of the war, the Japanese language had not been in use, so we had to start the teaching of Japanese from scratch. It was very difficult to try to return to a normal pre-war level.

But in this post-war period an interesting thing was that in addition to children of Japanese descent, non-Japanese children also began to come. There was one Caucasian child whose parents were public school teachers. There was also a young haole teacher from the mainland teaching at Naalehu public school who wanted to learn conversational Japanese. She too came to register. The Japanese that this teacher learned was immediately used by her with ease in greetings and simple conversation. With such expanded interest, the reopening of the Japanese language school was a very happy one for everyone.

As soon as possible my husband took the proposal for the reconstruction of Pahala Hongwanji to the members and they approved the plan. Mr. Hashimoto, the president

69

of Naalehu Hongwanji, at once called a meeting to which were invited the advisors, and the executive board members of the two temples. About twenty of them met for the first time at the Naalehu minister's residence for discussion. Someone said, "first of all, let's agree on recording our individual financial pledges in the donation book." That suggestion was unanimously applauded and approved, but for a while no one made a move to be the first to sign the book. Perhaps everyone felt the gravity of the responsibility in being the first person recorded on the list. Then suddenly Mr. Tanaka stood up and said, "It seems the big land owners and high salaried persons present seem to hesitate to sign first. It is presumptuous of me but I pledge $ ____, which is the most that I can do within my ability. I humbly request that the rest of you do the same and individually donate the greatest amount you can within your own capabilities." He said this very forcefully. Everybody applauded. At once everyone wrote on the records. It was a very lively start! The brand new car belonging to Isakichi Hashimoto, the president of the Kyodan, which was used to solicit donations, was practically worn out by the rough usage over the bumpy roads. My husband was very much moved by the cooperation of the members and he recorded his gratigude in his memoirs. The details are included in his posthumous collected works so I shall omit them here.

# Looking Back

HALF A CENTURY ago Naalehu roads were covered with rocks and holes. Driving was difficult. I experienced many traffic accidents myself. Once it happened on the way to school. The car we were riding almost went over the cliff. We three (my husband, Akira, and I) had a narrow escape. After that, Akira became afraid of riding in a car. For this reason, my husband and I went to school leaving Akira alone at home. Whenever we left Akira he always ran out to the gate saying, "Mother, please come back alive!" and he waved his hands. I clearly remember Akira waving his hands and hear his piping voice as if it were just yesterday.

There are many things and events that should be recorded. Such as the ultimely death of Bishop Yemyo Imamura who expended much concern and effort in the training of nisei ministers and the development of English propagation programs. I would have liked also to record the wonderful dedication of the nisei minister and Caucasian minister and their great sacrifices and hardships. But since these matters are recorded in greater detail in other publications, I shall with one exception limit myself to the above recollections of a missionary's wife. I should like to add here that the

Reverend Ernest Hunt brought the light of hope to the Honpa Hongwanji Mission of Hawaii through his great effort in English propagation. Also, not only before the war but during the war years, there were many unheralded persons throughout the islands who stood as guardians of the Dharma at the various temples and who served successfully in propagation of the teachings.

After my husband's retirement we said farewell to the island of Hawaii and moved to Honolulu. We lived at the minister's residence at McInerny *fukyojo* (branch temple). I was offered a teaching position at Palama Gakuen, to which I commuted and taught Japanese language. Until the day of my husband's death we had visitors practically every day and I had a lively and fruitful life.

Presently, my body has become weaker. I am living at the nursing home, but many people come and visit me and I am overwhelmed. Besides, I am at ease because my only son Akira stays with me everyday. "Mother, please live long, there is nothing to worry," he tells me tenderly. My daughter-in-law also came from the mainland and nursed me and made me happy. My grandchildren also think and worry about me. I do not know how to thank them, and the Reverend and Mrs. Kawaji, Mr. and Mrs. Albert Shimizu, and others that I have troubled. They were all very helpful to me.

My day is getting closer to return to the Pure Land and I have asked Reverend Kawaji for a favor about this book. After ninety odd years in this world, I owe many thanks to many people who helped me in so many ways. I would like to dedicate this book to everybody, with many thanks. I really wanted to identify their names individually, however, there are so many that in case I miss some names it will be unfair. So I should like to again thank every one of you from the bottom of my heart.

With Gassho,<br>
Shigeo Kikuchi (Author).

# Other Books That Will Enhance Your Understanding of Shin Buddhism

*Buddha and Man,* Eikichi Ikeyama - the cosmopolitan east/west approach of Ikeyama, one of the first Japanese Buddhists to teach and translate in Europe is a refreshing, non-scholarly, direct approach to confronting the meaning of one's life. This vivid translation by Dr. Toshikazu Arai is the first of Ikeyama's works to appear in English. 62 pages.
ISBN-0-938474-09-X . . . . . . . . . . quality paperback, $6.95

*The Path of Awakening,* Kosho Soga - dharma essays by a 'thirty-something' author that cover the range of everyday experience with Buddhist insights that are joyous and clear. 63 pages.
ISBN-0-938474-07-3 . . . . . . . . . . . . . . . . . . . . . . . . . $6.95

*Ajatasatru,* The Story of Who We Are by Shoji Matsumoto and Ruth Tabrah- the absorbing story of the Nirvana sutra and Shinran's comments on using the drama of this ancient Indian prince to see ourselves as we are today. Clear and simple language gives a powerful picture of the reality of being human. 71 pages.
ISBN-0-938474-08-1 . . . . . . . . . . . . . . . . . . . . . . . . . $6.95

*Shoshinge,* the heart of Shin Buddhism, by Dr. Alfred Bloom, Dean of the Institute of Buddhist Studies, Berkeley, California. Bloom is at his best in this very readable commentary on the modern relevance of the Shin Buddhist way of life and thought. Contains Nagatani/Tabrah translation of Shin's basic chant, Shinran's Shoshinge. 108 pages.
ISBN-0-938474-06-5 . . . . . . . . . . . . . . . . . . . . . . . . . $6.95

*Tannisho,* a Shin Buddhist Classic, translated by Dr. Taitetsu Unno of Smith College with an 'afterword' explaining the experience and insights of Shin in everyday life. Popular college text. 73 pages.
ISBN-0-938474-04-9 . . . . . . . . . . . . . . . . . . . . . . paper, $6.95
ISBN-0-938474-05-7 . . . . . . . . . . . . . . . hardcover, $12.95

*Resource for Modern Living: Tannisho* by Dr. Alfred Bloom, a popular commentary that links modern life and its problems with the timeless solutions offered in Shinran's classic text. 102 pages.
ISBN-0-938474-00-6 . . . . . . . . . . . . . . . . . . . . . . . . . $6.95

*Bodhisattvas Everywhere* by T. Sakakibara, 90 year old master of 1000 year old Jojuji Temple near Kyoto discusses current topics like genetic engineering, war, violence in the schools, from a Buddhist point of view. 63 pages.
ISBN-0-938474-03-0 .......................... $6.95

*The Buddhist World of Awakening* by Takamaro Shigaraki. The freshness, candor, and deep sincerity of this popular writer lead readers to new levels of understanding the basic concepts of Shin as the exciting horizon of Mahayana Buddhism. Widely used as text for individual and class study of Buddhism. 86 pages.
ISBN-0-938474-02-2 .......................... $6.95

*One Man's Journey* by Kazuo Miyamaoto. The delightful spiritual autobiography of a Japanese-American physician who wins the heart of readers with his confessions of being a sentimentalist who "cries at sad movies" and "gets a headache, becomes tired and confused" when he reads philosophical treatises. A frank account of Buddhist life. 120 pages.
ISBN-0-938474-01-4 .......................... $6.95

*Introduction To Shin Buddhism* by T. Shigaraki, a short, easy-to-read analysis of what Shin Buddhism is and the kind of future it may provide followers. 29 pages.
Pamphlet ................................... $2.95

*Shin Sutras To Live By*, an inspirational handbook of Shin Buddhist chants, rituals, and homages for everyday use and study. 45 pages.
ISBN-0-938474-12-X .......................... $3.95
Audiotape also available ..................... $2.95


Available from Buddhist Study Center Press
Order Dept: Kyodan Bookstore
1727 Pali Highway
Honolulu, Hawaii 96813


Please enclose check or money order. Include $3.00 for postage and handling. Standard discount schedules for text adoptions.